120 Days of Poetry

Illustrated by Naomi Muñoz Fantauzzi

Author's Note

This book doesn't adhere to any style or rule; rather, it serves as an embodiment of emotions spanning across 120 days. I composed this book during a challenging phase of my life when I experienced a whirlwind of words within me, yearning to be released. With each passing day, I channeled these distinct emotions dedicating each day to a specific feeling.

First Thought

Explosion of stars in the sky expresses my love
Look up, see my love falling from above
I wake up, my first thought is you, a morning dove
Falling for you is easy as slipping on a glove

I would keep fighting, even if struck by thunder
I would search the entire earth, left to wander
Alive in eternity, there would be no other
For you, my heart will always hunger

Listen to my words and believe
Your heart, I will never deceive
You will never see my love leave
I might be naive, but your love is my relief.

Show You

I will hold you when the world drowns you
In each other's embrace, we'll feel like we flew
When our eyes lock, you will see my words are true
My love on all roads, leaving a clue

My warmth will take away your pain
Moon as my judge, this love is not vain
At full speed my feelings hit you like a train
All your fears, with my sword, will be slain

This sadness running your veins, I transfuse to me
Help break the chains of suffering, be free
The screams and whispers, all a silent plea
Your hand in mine will make wonders like the sea.

No Fright

Facing the sky, I see the stare of the stars
I feel my heart, opening up the scars
Gravity can't hold me, I float to mars
I say goodbye as I write my last memoirs

The sun reminds me of a smile
Where I could get lost for miles
Everything was worthwhile
Shards of your light I need to compile

Drifting away, I start to lose sight
In me there is no fright
I'm getting closer to the night
An image of you keeps my eyes bright.

A Little While

No matter where in the world
No matter where in the universe
No matter if in this life or the next
I will eternally love you

Even if all that's left is pain
Even if I have nothing to gain
Even if madness takes over my brain
I will find your heart and sustain

I will give you the light of the moon
Will show you what it is to be swoon
To other hearts I will be immune
Just hold on a little while, I'll be there soon.

Stay Kind

When you are cut too deep with lies
Look at the truth, just open your eyes
Right above you, the most amazing skies
No need for those painful cries

Listen to the whispers in the wind
They bring what you are trying to find
Somewhere on the horizons it will be defined
No need for the unkind, stay kind.

Steal

Your touch takes me to heaven
Your warmth is my personal haven
If I can't hold your hand, I feel uneven
In your infinite heartbeat, I would breakeven

My ink, your name, with every stroke I heal
With every letter speaking loud as any peal
My will stronger than the toughest steel
For my entire universe you steal.

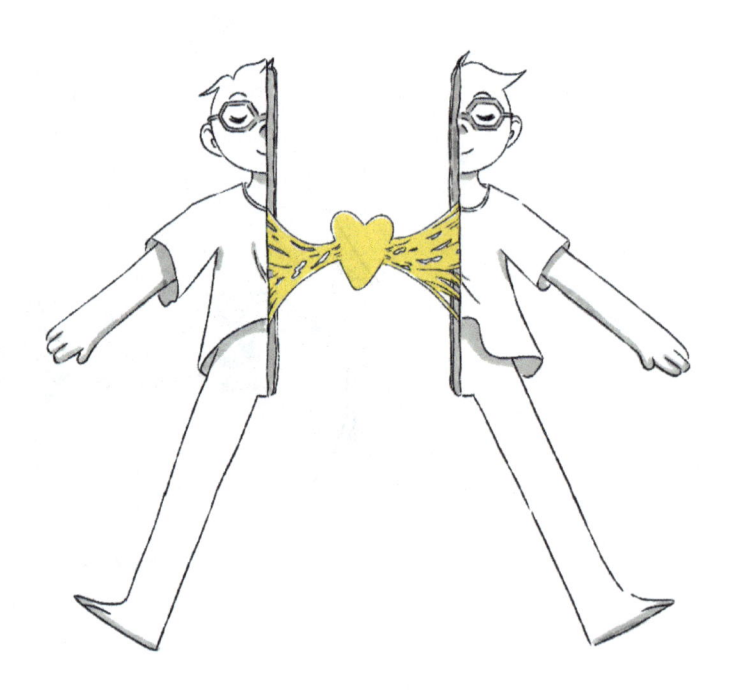

Hope

In the cosmos they hear my scream
More like a nightmare than a dream
Wanting to become a star feels extreme
In the end, I can see the brightest gleam

I hear my breath fainting
My life, I can see it as a painting
My body feels like it's fading
With my heart, hope I'm creating.

Reveal

At the horizon you can see my shine
The stars at night reveal the sign
Life's winds of destiny complete our trine
Fate has us tangled in its unique vine

Written in the skies with a wand
An undeniable bond
Magnificently overfond
The galaxy will respond.

Do Not Fall

Such tragedies circling, I wish they abate
We could all unite, we can change our fate
Wonderous energy that lives inside makes us great
Open the gate in our hearts, let's throw away the hate

Confront darkness, stop the behavior that is aberrant
Become free from the negative embrace, be transparent
When in the garden of confusion, you feel things are errant
Find strength of love and kindness, don't fall in front of a tyrant.

Make It

Everything feels cold as ice
Scavenging for answers like mice
Throwing my chances like dice
Will anything ever suffice?

A purpose sweet and smooth like cream
Refusing an abyss that seems dim
Nothing is sure or how it should seem
With an iron hope, I won't run out of steam.

Friend

Rare as the northern lights is our friendship
Born apart with an iron kinship
A bond indestructible beyond partnership
Sailing adventures, dreams set ship

Lucky to uncover this rare find
So much treasure in one person so kind
Our lives would cross paths even if blind
Remaining strong every year in heart and mind.

Father

Grateful for all the work
No matter how many times you rework
You tried your best to nurture your artwork
Always gave a smirk in front of any quirk

With all the experience you gathered
You showed me what really mattered
In front of you, nothing could shatter
No matter if you stumble, you're the best father.

At Least

Can I make my home in the clouds
Far away from the crowds
Let the sky cover me in its shrouds
Until the winds start to get wildly loud

Reach my hand to grasp the sun
Thinking today is the day I might have won
When I think I'm done, and things seem dun
I end on the clouds and say, at least it was fun.

Wake

The day you let go of my hand, I floated to outer space
Searching for your love, I wonder was it worth the race?
You leave your trace in me, all I can see is your face
You always were my only ace, my one true grace

The galaxy can hear the sound of my heartbreak
Each step I take, every breath I make, is a small ache
Letting every bit of hope be at stake with no brake
With the fallen aftermath, my eyes wake.

Once

It's a wonder how the light in my heart absconded
Not giving my other senses a chance to have responded
Until the dare to feel this gift, my heart was reminded
Took a while to get here, but life always corresponded

Touching the vibrant miracles around me, I must accolade
To believe that once I walked the road blindly strayed
Afraid of the light that brimmed in me, I hid in the shade
Now the sunlight that plays around me is everything I prayed.

When

When you are feeling acerbic
When defenses are as cold as the Antarctic
When you lose sight and become frenetic
Remember you were born to be majestic

Look at the colors of life, don't be so critical
Follow the musical heart, don't be so analytical
Take breaths of beauty that feel mystical
In the hug of life you see we are nothing typical.

Legendary

It's a beautiful pain when I get close to your flame
Once our worlds collide, we become one and the same
Every feeling tangible, I can almost put them in a frame
A tearful ghost of you, the saddest shame

Sometimes the black hole of doubt seems scary
The magic our hearts provide is not ordinary
Even if underground, it's something nobody can bury
After life, it continues to live, becoming legendary.

Light

Light of day, light of night, light of my eyes, my only light
Your waves of fire crash on me, not even the sun is as bright
Came unexpectedly, racing through my atmosphere like a meteorite
You're my sunset, you're my sunrise, becoming my infinite twilight

Big Bang in my heart as you rise, a new universe in me appears
Impacted by this new worlds in me, shaped like mysterious spheres
I ponder, will it still gravitate around me for many years?
Growing within a new universe, staring at lights, wishing it never clears.

Closer

Mesmerized by waves of your lava red hair
It stops my breath and compresses all the air
In all my travels, I have never found anything so rare
Daring to approach with care the brightest flare

Pulling closer to dangers surrounding your charm
I dodge burning troubles, promising you no harm
All the heavy wisps are gone in my sanctuary arms
Let the erupting defenses down, together we disarm.

Adventure

Protected by nature's cowl
Mysterious movements of owl
The forest starts to howl
Silent sounds like growls

Can't see the sky from such high trees
I can hear bees traveling on the breeze
Senses unknown in this adventure's tease
Keep walking new soil even if I fall at my knees

Leaves sing me a song
Earth maintains my stance strong
Wind show me direction, no matter how long
Sun show me light even when I'm wrong.

Sister

Mother's love, best friend's trust, the clasp of a sister
When things seem abolished in an endless twister
In pain, her healing sounds make it with a whisper
In straps of shadows, her hand reaches with such a glister

Becoming the vault of my every confession
With your smile, you take away depression
Covering me in the cloth of forgiveness without question
When walking roads of madness, you maintain discretion.

Mom

You're my mother earth
Gifting me love since birth
The joy you unearth
Every delight you make worth

With every mother's kiss
You make my heart bliss
Care that saves me from abyss
A privilege being your son, thank you for this.

Brother

Remembering knocking my brother's door
Admiring, will I be like that from the floor
Looking for the path, wanting to be more
Creating a loving brother's war

Growing up, understanding brother's will
Acquiring experience from every skill
Angry from sad, sad from happy, it was a thrill
Acquiring strength to make it up life's hill.

Pollution

Stardust falls, make your roots grow, hello nature
Dimming light rebirths life, spectacular creature
Sky and oceans reflect a beautiful feature
Atmosphere embracing with nurture

Privilege to be part of this grand contribution
The ocean lights show me the solution
Mellow grass speaks to me absolution
Conclusion of hearts drumming, end of pollution.

Butterfly

Aspiration of a butterfly
Fighting time as I fly
With every flap, sound amplifies
To tumble, I will always deny

Journey made to vanish
Ten days, refuse to perish
Short or long, willed not to banish
Hopeful wings can manage.

Escape

Disorientated eyes, opening is a sting
Pain mocks me, like it could sing
Hope gone in a snowstorm, never to see spring
Mind covered in needles that stop anything

Dreaming faith is a sudden pang
Running endlessly, stabs like a boomerang
Thoughts escaping depths of a boundless clang
Can I escape this harm before I hear the bang?

Sparrow

Dearest, I'm sorry for the teardrop
All that sadness, wish I could stop
Let me hold you while gasping last sob
Your teardrop gives my heart raindrops

Let me wipe away that sorrow
Show you the magic of tomorrow
Leap forward on this joyful arrow
Let your hardship fly like sparrows.

Story

Tell me a story from one of your books
Where dreams come true, no matter the looks
You keep getting up when thrown fiery hooks
Even get the girl when hands get terrible spooks

A world hidden inside infinite pages
Touching the imagination of any ages
Helping weave the careful thread in life's stages
Leaving blockhead, making me wise as sages.

Diamond

Diamond skies show me the rainbow
Diamond Sea show me how wishes flow
Diamond winter show me love can melt snow
Diamond world shows how beautiful is your glow

How precious to be alive
A treasure to have drive
Fortune to see beauty and dive
Such wealth just to survive.

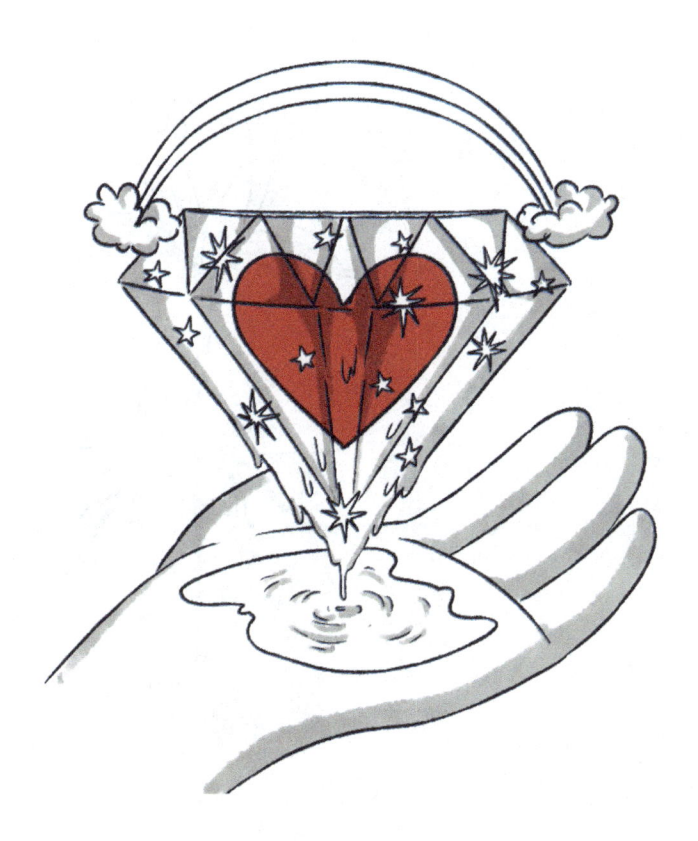

Astounded

Your love started as a seed
With care, it grew with great speed
Stronger even when you bleed
Its life force became your creed

A tree of passion surrounded
With one kiss, you founded
With that, every inch was bounded
Breathtaking, even heaven is astounded.

Memory

Your light entwines in a photograph
Forecasting my emotions, I get a laugh
Memories of you being my other half
Sentimental whirlwind writing your epitaph

Like a picture taken, your gone in an instant
If I knew, even to time I would have been resistant
With your image in my hand, wish I was not distant
Living locked moments of when we were existent.

Wish

Uncontrollable breath of night
Feel the bite of the starry wolf's might
Be my natural moon satellite
You capture what's left of my light

Shadows grow in dusk before nightfall
In those final moments, the sky starts to call
I try to climb over this imaginary wall
Wishing I could run eternally like a waterfall.

Admire

In her eyes I see the stars
Universe you hide in magical jars
Her melodious voice like tuned guitars
Pulse breaking speed limits like cars

Body pulls me away like a wave
Your secrets, I'll take to the grave
Even in distance, her I would save
To her study I become a slave.

Not Lost

Wandering around the hands of juncture
I see life's events in the form of sculpture
Finding myself lost in the fruits of culture
Something recreates a way of structure

Witness clockwork in my eye's mechanism
Greatness you can see through the heart's prism
Attracted to the mysteries of life like magnetism
In adventures, you can still find heroism.

The Forgotten

Let me travel through skies luster
Where hope and dreams cluster
Once set eyes, it's hard not to fluster
Where no matter the journey, we bluster

Voyage to the untold stories
Seeking fate's riddle for glories
A feat to complete for no worries
One day, words will fly out from these diaries.

Faith

Can you embrace me with your trust
Yearn for a glimpse before I turn to dust
My faithful words travel like a gust
In my knees, my hands turn to rust

A sign of illuminance that I long
Time passes like flashes, yet I remain strong
Waiting for the stars to perform their song
End this timeless eclipse, show me I'm wrong.

Across The River

You had a house across the river
I would visit from the other side
Your golden hair, like a fairytale shimmer
Locked my eyes, falling in love's tide

I could sit and talk to you
My voice sounding like fireworks
Expressing how deeply I felt
By having you so close to me

The moon's light danced upon the river
As if tiny stars were falling just for us
I would collect a glass of wishing stars
Each night they'd remind me of you

One starless night, I was left alone
Where we used to be side by side
Every day, I whisper to the water
To bring you back, to bridge the divide.

Your Sound

Lost in the sound of your guitar strings
Surprised by the serenity it brings
Finding my way when your voice sings
With every note, all worries take wings

Make my bed out of your melodies
A cure for every scar, my remedies
Could something hide with such rarities
Each sound, my personal therapy.

Wolf

Howl at the drums of my heartbeats
Trying to walk, but my legs run the streets
Breathing becomes soft the more it heats
Seeking moon and stars before violent meets

Away from the pack of humanity
Keeping the wolf in me from vanity
My spirit seeks the aurora of sanity
In a globe that turns with insanity.

Thoughts

Scratches in the depths of my brain
Waiting on angel's light to break the chain
At the vein of madness, I ponder its gain
Explosions of screams that bring bane

Clear drops fall from space
Will I ever win this race?
See finally my true face
Could hell ever find grace?

Silent Scream

Walking the streets astray finding home in the shadows
My heartbeat rushes as it absorbs fear that shatters bones
Surrounded by the eyes of blackness that hover around me
Light fades through the tunnel of my eyes, sinking in dampness

Reach my hand out whispering silent screams to the echoes unheard
Fingertips play the air with faith like a musical prayer that falls unvoiced
Sunken, slowly wondering do I still breathe, seconds pass like lost years
Reacting to unbelievable sounds of blood making its path to my heart

Nerves waiting patiently for the last gasp of help that my hope has
My eyes open but closed by the pitch black that has drowned me
Last bit of strength I scream between worlds, scream a desperate rope
Sounds like a roar viciously eternal like an animal cornered to fight

Suddenly I awaken to the sunlight finding its dance around my body
Angelic reflections of light bouncing around me like smiles in a dream
Fresh new gusts of air fill my lungs, feel like freedoms sweet inhale
A day like a painting residing in my iris, telling a story left to unwind.

Farewell

Your radiant smile, a gateway to bliss
Hard to believe such brilliant light exists
Hair so magical, at every wave I'm lifted
Clear eyes like an ocean, I float in wonder
Tell me, how I came across true treasure?

Danced like flowers in the wind
Mesmerizing with every delicate move
To believe you are my impossible tower
The sun blinding me to see my dream
I can just close my eyes and climb

Following the beauty of your steps
How marvelous to see its progress
Leaving a mark that is remembered
Where generations will follow with pride
I will be a guard of the love you've created

Once it's over, I'll kiss your eyes so you can rest
I will hold your hand until the last sounds
Forever grateful of every breath you take
Saying last words in front of your favorite tree
The sea as witness, I will say goodbye, my love.

One

One second, I'm in love with life
One minute, I exist for this love
One hour, I fight for a place in eternity
One day, I'm defined by the choices
One month, surprised by surroundings
One year, lost in this insanity

Time clock arms send me in reverse
Madness that destroys what I cherish
Each passing moment breaks my reality
Can hardly see the clear sky anymore
Amidst the fire fueled by silence
With guilty eyes that were closed

Ground speak to me of your pain
Wind, tell me your stories
Trees, share with me your suffering
Ocean scream to me crimes
That cannot be erased
Leaning towards the question, is there hope?

Moving On

The aroma of your perfume transports me to another world
A place we are together and the flame of us burns louder
My roots were firmly planted in your heart, nourishing our love
Reliving the crystal-smooth sands where we lay with daydreams
Stories of us where we could happily leap between every word

Now days are colder, no fire to spark the heat to feel alive
Upon the weathered pages of letters written with a melancholic pen
Here I stand, enveloped in emptiness, feeling the void that surrounds me
Waiting for the day when that familiar scent embraces me once again
Engulfing senses, words spoken will resound. "I have forgotten you."

Despair

Finding purpose on an uncertain globe, devoid of nourishment
Like hidden quartz in stones, I am a mystery to the unknown
When my hands can't form a fist, they cry out to the surface
Breathing in the twilight, where my soul is measured
Let the shadow companion that follows me take over last blooms

Look out the windows that showcase the darkest movies
Where flowers will never witness the day that brings life
Where the sun won't bounce off our skin and sing
When little ones shed tears heavier than rocks
Scenes of hugs and love with hidden murders in embrace

Hear my sigh, long and low, filled with sadness
Explosions of despair amplified, thousands of miles from me
Making their way slowly in front of me to bare
Fruits of hope falling rotten from the branches of dreams
Here we remain, still waiting for the endless end.

Appreciate

Drinking moonlight's waterfall from cracks in the sky
Let life run through my veins, telling secrets to my blood
Moving branches speak to me, revealing signs of truth
My open heart continues to beat in the clear air
Some sort of love hidden within the trails of leaves

Guided by the arrows of this old compass
Every direction leads me to adoration
Spring's music of newborns
Summer's clasp of warmth
Autumn's end and begging of life
Winter's cold tears

Let newly blossomed flowers be the light in your eye
The melting snow be a shower of factualness
The warm sun ignites the burning passion within us
Howl of wolves be cries that reach the unheard
Faded rainbows fight to show us the path
One right step can plant seeds of hope
Let me wrap you in my sky so you can feel.

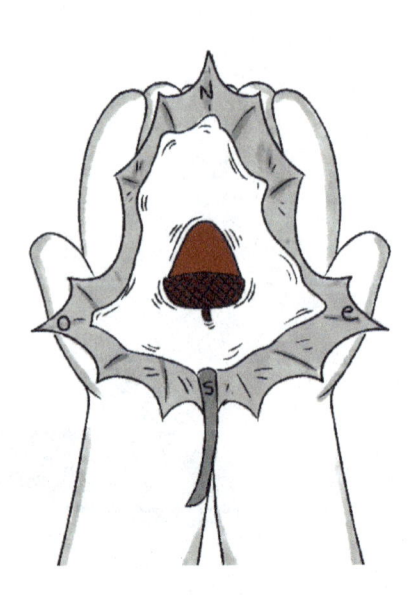

I Love You

I love you beyond comprehension to any mind
I love you in front of any obstacles created
I love you not knowing how it came to be
I love you without prideful chains
I love you without poisonous doubts
I love you without any devils in my eyes
I love you here and now, effortlessly
I love you with inks eternal calligraphy
I love you even when there's a specter of you
I love you when I remember your joyful smile
I love you when you're the center of my embrace
I love you with every visit to my heart
I love you even after I lay a flower on the ground.

Only You

Only you are the dreams of my future
My timeless love, you are the battery of my life

My lustrous river of passion where only we can dance
I will whirl you through its waters in shadow or light

My moving flame, my moonlight queen
The ageless sky showers me in stars

Forever imprinted in my eyes
Only you are the world that spins around me.

Until Then

I wait for you like a hand waiting to be held
Until then my hand wanders lost
I wait for you like lips waiting to be kissed
Until then they just long for your name
I wait for you like paint for canvas
Until then it drips in torment

My soul aches until you knock its door once again
From its lonesome bellow, it calms at your sight
Footprints of you reside on all paths of my mind
At night, my eyes project memories of you
Like a sad story waiting for its happy ending
Until then, here I write with ink made of tears.

Home

I cannot fight the pull of your existence
Flying me to you, landing in all your stars
When I fall into the ocean of your love
It drifts me to the isles of your heart
Welcoming me like an old friend
I build a house with nails of our union
Window's view of a beautiful us

I can now look at your alluring eyes
I see the reflection of where I want to stay
With bravery thickening the air in my lungs
Gibberish finds its composure in my mouth
From south to north, my head rises
Strong and powerful like thunderstorms
Yet delicate as a soft caress upon the cheek
Here are my words: I love you.

Struggle

Trapped in dark words made from shadows
A hollow core born from the gut, spreading through my body
All abstractions of despair crawl their way around my brain
Will I ever take flight? Spread broken wings and find light
My soul fades on blackened fire, let ashes be my curtains

Hear the songs that slither to my ears with lyrical lunacy
Bells that sound like heartbeats overpowering the senses
Screams vocalize, muting soundwaves to an empty world
I stream endlessly, dividing me in two until it finds its edge
Can hear the flutter of raven's wings looking to save me

My body itches like flesh made of bugs
Hand on my chest trying to find the blaze
Illuminate penumbra from the appellation of my life
Trying to find the gate of ebullience in my eyes
So I can witness this endless fight.

Traces

Memories of how, with one gaze, you made a nervous heart stand still
How I could see a map of the universe in your face with a single smile
Being close to you was like floating through the Milky Way in awe
Your soul a bright palette of unimaginable colors for the eyes

Your kiss, like a supernova, consumed me completely in its romance
A hug, like wrapping me in its cosmic web, my heart felt alive
Our fingers intertwining like playful stars finding their perfect place
Open your eyes, like two shooting stars, a wonder to spectate

I feel you traveling my memories, making your way even in my dreams
At night, my heart becomes the brightest embers keeping me warm
Your stardust makes its way through my body, igniting the light
Traces of your voice echo in my ear, bringing calmness to the soul

Now my kisses fall into black holes, searching for your lips
My hands fade from the world, looking for a perfect place in yours
Gravity fails me, for you are the sun, my world revolves around
Memories of you are all my galaxies reflecting your form.

Met You

Everything I tasted turned to ash before I met you
Music was silent to me, just passing by my ears
Words were mute; they fell unheard from mouths
The smell of flowers disappeared as I approached

The sun was hidden in the basement of my eyes
Before I met you, stars concealed with cloth of night
The moon was just an eclipse that blinded me
Before I met you, clouds were a fog around my heart

Seasons where forgotten, time lost its way
Waterfalls lost their voice, trees lost their dance
The ground was not where my weight delivered me
Before I met you, air was the sand of my lungs

Everything was unknown, a fallen world
You opened the door to my eyes, letting light in
I met you, your beauty made my world known
I finally heard when you spoke, I saw the seasons.

Do

Tears of a man who never knew the road to travel
They fall like drops that never found their ocean
Who never knew beauty of different color skies
Suffered from a world of black and white

A man that never felt crashing waves of the sea
An incomplete body missing its puzzle piece
Absence of welcoming landscapes
Never got a chance to paint the mind

He who never takes the direction of risk
Looses threads of emotions that form life
He who never roams the sky
Cannot know the caress of the air

A man who does not journey world's terrain
Can never feel the loudest capacity of his heart
To live is to explore depiction of the world
Dream outside the sleeping world of lost tears.

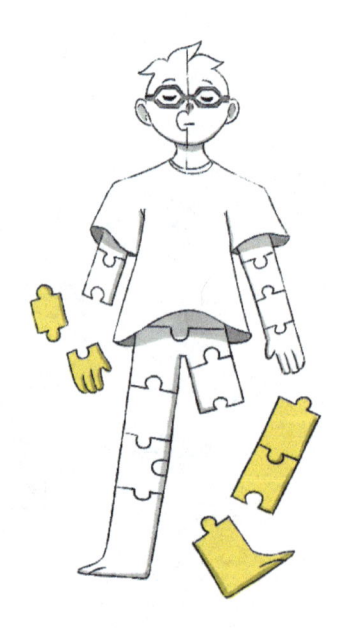

Blessing

Soften smile brought incalculable joy to hidden hearts
The day you were born, a new star appeared in the sky
Tiny hands have the world spinning around its fingers
Little heartbeat with such loud roars to share on earth

Tiniest feet never looked so big, waiting to make their imprint
Beyond ocean and sky, everything will learn your name
New luminous eyes adapting to new wondrous light
The shape of rainbows you will see will inspire your soul

Even your cries make the unluckiest days the luckiest of them
Such bright energy, like a living aurora surrounding my nights
Hopeful dreams formed in reality, filling every vacant part of me
Like a fairytale full of astonishments, I now carry a true miracle.

Hidden Love

Let me save you before the rocks crumble down
I know you prefer armor instead of a gown
Let me protect you here, even in front of the town
I know you love me even if you think I'm a clown

Whispers of offense rise upon us until we drown
Between the shadows, I steal a kiss until sundown
Hidden lovers with eyes that follow all around
Bodies destined since we could touch the ground

For us, I would fight all kingdoms until I'm renowned
When pushed to my knees, I refuse to be knocked down
Until we can walk together, autumns burning browns
Until then, my blood falls on steel for your crown.

Run

Run a mile, run a marathon, to reach your kiss
Run to the edge of earth where it ends and it starts
My lips to reach your lips would create a new world
Where you and I reside, creating landscapes of love

Running through water to reach your kiss
I can see the sun in the lining of your lips
Guiding my nights, calling me to its warmth
Ever so close to the firestorm of your kisses

Ran for days, days seemed like years, here I am
Across storms and walls, I'm here to claim my gem
To show you the last kiss you will ever need
With its final touch, I complete this wedlock.

Never

From all the hearts in this world I chose your wild heart
Full of curiosity for life's mysteries hidden all around
Energy waiting to burst out like a turned-on engine
Even when standing still, it looks like your about to run

You love to take deep breaths of hope for the next day
Feeling sand at the beach, purifying your skin
Still loving to climb trees for a different view
You walk looking up, wondering beyond the sky

You look at me like the first time you felt love
Holding my hand like it was your personal sanctuary
Every kiss is like it was your first and last one
I could never imagine choosing another heart like yours.

The Reason

Even if my eyes were to lose sight, never to see light again
I would still find you and choose only you, even in the dark
My hands only crave the soothing feel of your flesh
Without every inch of you, I lose the sense of touch

The taste of your lips, an instant taste of euphoria
Stripping me away from them puts my joy in dormancy
Your fragrance hypnotizes me in a loop of beautiful memories
When it vanishes, the reminiscence becomes empty torment

Hearing your voice is to love; I could never find another guide
Falling deaf to your sound would be agonizing romance
Discovering the world with you is like finding heaven at my side
The image of you not being here is like being lost in limbo

It does not matter how I used to love in the shadow of the past
It has no importance how others build love; you are my fortress
Watching you, hearing you, seeing you, admiring you endlessly
You are the yearning reasons for being in love.

Artist

My admiration falls in amazement as you paint the world
Brushstrokes made of bravery as you fight through the colors
Like surfing the rainbows to your goals, people fall in wonderment
Mixing paint of emotions you come out with the most grand tones

Eyes that can see the unseen, capturing true beauty in front of them
An artist made of every shade in our spinning sphere of life
Being around you feels like being sucked in to a new reality
Wish to be part of the blend, making my existence in your canvas.

Agony

The cut of pain makes a river flow with agony
Burning wings become ashes as they fly away
Tears vaporize before they fall, keeping their secrets
Climbing barbed wire of survival to the top of living

Walking in quicksand to find the shadow of a dream
Keyless life to the doors of this cycle of disenchantment
Crunching of nervous fingers becoming tied to write truth
Desperate heart finding its way out so it can finally breath

Vitality that makes everything bloom feeds with every smile
All you see are frowns of the broken hidden under masks
Fragments of glee shatter more after every walked mile
Battling every conjured monster to not be another heaven's file.

Passion

I will cover you in the quilted sheets of passion
Love falling around the curves of your waist
Feeling the heat of our romance being born
Ours has no caption, an enigma that can't be torn

Seizing the moment that completes my cosmos
My feet touching yours, making a boundless dance
The flavor of your skin invades my palette, leaving me entranced
Fingers running through your hair like pilgrims discovering

Hands clasp, creating a lock of intimacy with no key
Your warm breath melting the ice of my vital force
Our spirits playing with each other like two wild wolves
Powerless in the gaze of our eyes, mirroring our fate.

No Matter

It does not matter from what part of the world you are
I can see how breathtaking your presence is, like magic
A miraculous star leaving traces everywhere it travels
Healing any lingering scars around the world

Kiss me once, its memory forever embedded in my heart
Leaving your mark while you sail in the ocean of my love
Like a dart, you go straight for the bullseye of anyone's joy
Close my eyes, I dream of you; open my eyes, you are right here

Your pictures like untold letters that reach me through the waves
A smile so beautiful, like a garden of roses blooming for the first time
Every action made spreads kindness in people's eyes, creating belief
No matter your name or who you are today, my nature is to love you.

Fools Race

Trying to find the moment where my legs got lost
Felt the sweat of pain drip down my face as I exhaust
My field of vision blinded by life's unforgiving frost
To locate the invisible direction, there's a cruel cost

Going through a wall of fog in front of me, wondering am I breathing
Completing a dream with sharp pieces, is it worth bleeding
Watching the rain fall in a lonely city leaves my eyes grieving
Does any of my heart's music have meaning? Or are its tunes leaving

Are the strings that play our destiny broken?
Can hear the screams of locked rooms unspoken
Strayed in false lights, tears become the token
My sun sleeps, waiting for the sunrise to be woken

All these false words splashed on my face
Turning me to an impostor's goal to chase
Pulling me out of place, stealing my grace
No longer ridiculed by the fool's race.

Cleanse

Cries of clouds dropped their tears on all the torn hearts
A sealed heaven leaving souls in a lost forest of affliction
A crack of hell surfaced, its flames slithering through the broken
Sufficing on flawed hopelessness of the muted and restrained

If all hands gather each other for the spread of love
All fractures that birth the obstruction of influence
Would withdraw their poison from the air that surrounds us
Let voices of every drop of rain cleanse the world.

My Queen

You are queen of my heart, ruling the kingdom of its pulsation
Walking its halls with such beauty, spreading your kindness
The purity of your love gives life to its grass, a magical reaction
Controlling the symphony of your own private concert inside

With every smile, you make your castle become larger
Every time you laugh the sky becomes brighter
Moments filled with pride sing out your name
Feeling blessed by arrows of love to call you my queen.

Stop

With heartless hands
You strangled my love
Hands with no remorse
Hands so depraved

A crime you escaped
With my tears as a trail
Caged in this pain
Waiting your next offense

Cold words like knives
Cut my life away
Stare that screams revile
Silences my thoughts

In my palm, I see the key
My mouth holds freedom
Soul that shouts bravery
With firm feet, I stop this odious.

Time

Such a young smile
Full of bright hopes
Stargazing dreams
Filled with nature's love

Time skips like flames
Adventuring the world
Taking foolish risks
Surfing winds in wonder

Clock arms run in circle
Old enough to be calm
To see truth behind lies
Finding wishes in kisses

Even if hours slip away
If the world is stone hard
Even if hands can't grasp
Dreams continue living on
Even if they don't come true.

Remember

Watching the spectrum
Through my glass eyes
Consuming white light
Shows me our forever

I can't help but wonder
If you will ever arrive
To the shore of my heart
Or is it a colorful illusion

Will I grow weary of waiting
Will I watch my hands wither
Before I see yours on top of mine
Is your heart fine, or is it blue

If I carve our name in timber
Will I remember them playing
If I gaze to salty seas
Will I recall my goodbye
Or will pages end in amnesia.

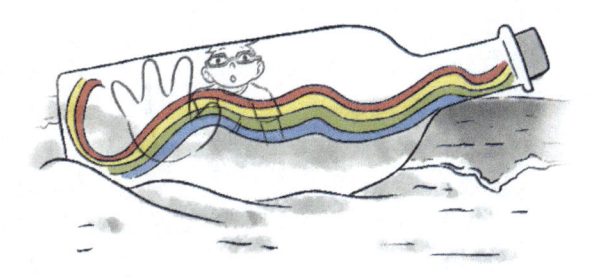

New Day

Good to see you again
My sun, warm guide
New day full of delight
Walking in the pleasures of you

I find reasons to smile
Pouring light of joy
Leafy concerts fly by
Skies clear away doubts

Clouds bloom with hope
Of a wonderful time
Don't cover those shining eyes
Experiences await for you

Going back to sleep
With a pillow of dreams
Can't wait to wake up
To yet another new day.

Homeless

You're like a ghost
That I wish would haunt me
An image that comes and goes

Floating around me
Making me nostalgic
Like a cherished souvenir

If your heart were touchable
I could have built a home
Now I'd rather be homeless.

A Shine

Our love like the moon
Has times when it shines
A quarter of a moment
And at times it's eclipsed

Like a curious twilight
Seeking a soft glow
No matter how low
There's always a next show

Even on pitch-black days
Like the moon at night
Love remains beautiful
Even if it's dead and lost.

Blind

I watched you with love
Saw your heart laugh
Admired your moves
Glanced at your rise

Witnessed your kindness
Judged when unkind
Viewed in spring of joy
Present in storms of tears

Attended the stories left to say
All lines had the same endings
That you will never be mine
I wonder how I stop being blind.

Liar

When the night Is silent,
Cheer your actions in your laugh
I will not sigh a word to the room

When you push it away,
My eyes will have the recording
In your reflection, you won't forget

In every heated sunrise,
I become more patient through the day
At cold sundown I expose the truth

In the safe space of lies,
You make your bed with treachery
There I wait, there I come for you.

Learning

Could not live in the world without wounds
Bruises that hurt my body but teach me
Bones that break but mend even stronger
Wounds that leave scars with stories to tell

A broken heart that cries blood
Becomes wiser after each drop
A tripped-overthinking mind
Finds new paths to search from

Without each destined pain
I would not have found you
Without every new changing tide
I could not keep you by my side.

My Answer

Like an exploding star
Even after its passing
My love keeps lucent
I hold it forever within me

Like a volcano's rupture
Running its lava down
Impossible to extinguish
Is my love with its heat

Even in slow death
I refuse to open its door
Until I fill your heart
With your every wish

My one and only girl
Beautiful as the seasons
My wish to every candle
Eons are short with you.

Maybe

I'll love her forever and always
Like lungs need oxygen
You keep my breathing steady
The salt to my life
Elevating every moment

You love him unconditionally
In the worst of fires
In the best of breezes
The strong branch
That holds the leaves together

But at the passing of sentiment
Of my old faded poems
I can still read the incomplete
Words that you used to complete
And wonder if it was never a maybe.

Brave

Fearful to say the words
That will change my seashore
Scared to have my first, last kiss
Terrified to let love thrum

To break the barriers of my brain
Fighting crowds that bury me
To write words of a poet's pen
Will change the spin of my world

To be free to hold you
The one that flew close
How hard it is to smile
Under a scream that loves

One day I won't ask myself why
Just move at its rhythm
I won't doubt my pen's thoughts
Will say with bold lines
You are my love.

Broke

I loved the way you fell asleep
With a tiny smirk on angelic face
How your breathing brought peace
I wondered about your dreams
I could only see your tranquility
Like a dandelion following the air

I loved when you looked at me
Capturing me like a photograph
How my days were complete
Because you hugged me tight
Each morning at first sunrise
Tip of your fingers on my face
Was all the hope I needed

When you walked out the door
Even after a needled goodbye
That pierced through my soul
After the curious tears that peek
On a saddened new world, I loved you
Even after my heart broke.

Over Me

If I could unravel the knots of this romance
I could had saved this heart from sinking
Instead, I miss every moment with each blink

I could had stopped the wall that divided us
With spoken remedies that could have healed
Now all I hear is the screech of "you are over me."

Forward

The cover you keep closed in your mind
Holds the most beautiful waiting stories
Until you open and start reading

Inhale these new words that give you freedom
Fly the paper airplane of ideas, be the pilot
Take steps towards the stairs of dreams.

Change

Won't let ghosts of the past consume me
In their vortex of repetition, making me tumble
Before the setting skies I find myself again

I hold the fire at night to find my way through
The louder my heartbeat the brighter the flame
An eruption of light unveils I'm not the same.

You and I

Wandered around the cold
All my life, as far as I remember
I would never have imagined
Your eyes would warm me
Like two flaming emeralds

Looked like mysterious magic
How you flew into my world
Landing at the center of my heart
Piercing the armor that guards it
Now feeling safer than ever

I don't feel the snow anymore
Just heated presence of you
My breath shows your name
Deep inside of me it's revealed
You are part of me, and I you.

Dormant

Impossible to walk this land
Wearing just one face to see
When every smile requires
Another set of intentions
Can one voice be enough?

Do we end up blinded
Fighting on the darkness
In a war we can't win
Stranded in our hearts
Where training begins

To discover the candles
That illuminate the halls
Of our wandering soul
Warriors lay dormant
Waiting to be awakened.

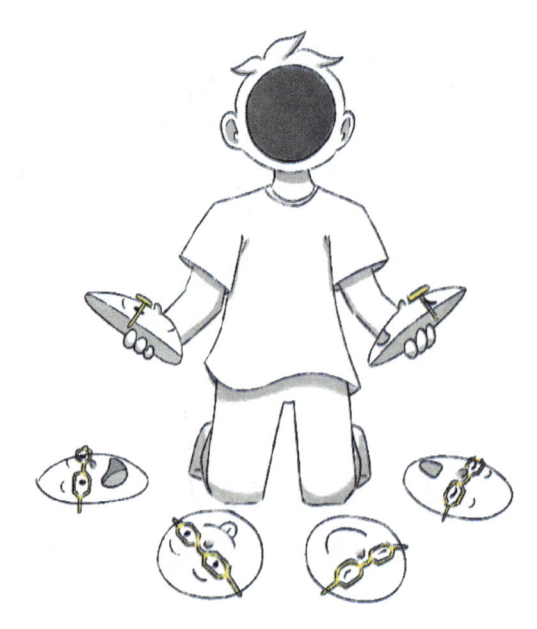

Lives

You are the angel of my demons
Rescued me from the dammed
Forgave my poisoned words
Lifted me from rocks that broke me

I will fight through land and sea
A thousand men cannot stop me
Nor the lashes from the sun
Or the cold lances of winter

I will protect you no matter where I am
I'm yours until my last remaining day
Even if the odds are covered with thorns
My love for you will live in life and death.

Here I Am

Abandoned in lion's mouth
Waiting to be devoured
By its shallow teeth
I escape their dangerous prison

To be found upside down
In my own reality
Where my blood finds fear
In the direction it runs

I struggle to not be lost
But I fight to find my feet
And find the way home
As I steady my stance
Filled with courage, here I am.

One Punch

Am I the hero of this story?
Will I fight the monsters?
Is one punch enough to win?
To defeat the broad dusk
That falls upon me

I must find the answers
To riddled question marks
That hunts my subconscious
I will be the feeling of fire
That never goes out

With a trained heart
I find the strength
In waves of my will
To never be still
I'm the hero of my story.

Never Give Up

Thunderous winds face me
They try to push me away
But my purpose is solid
I cut through the sounds
That spill through my body

The roar inside of me
Gives me the power
To battle for my cause
No matter how much I fall
The flash of light in me
Helps me get up once again

All the cries that clock in
Have made me stronger
To fight all the pains
That invade my heart's core
Even if my scars bleed
I will never give up.

Justice

A lesson of broken bones
Learned to transform pain
Into healing screams
From one heart to all
I command the stadium
Of crowds that rest in me

Explosions burst around me
Speeding massive fury
Righteousness in my eyes
Serves me as my shield
Against any hidden attack
That slips through the dark

A disciple of justice
Born from ones before me
Through ice and fire
I make my way through
All faceless villains
With one surge of truth.

Notebook

Trying to find answers
Between fantasy notebooks
And inked words of reality
Is there a way to save you
From the sinful apple
That has fallen upon you
Or will you see your light

The rollercoaster that rides
Through your intelligence
Clashes with the adversary
Waiting in the screen of your eyes
Making you madder to the names
That become blurred writing
My only desire is to rescue you

I know the letters that form
The horrid words made of voices
Are not the charming heart I know
But a fair illusion in your gravity
Fear not the world around you
Or what awaits beyond the sky
I still love with a fainted written name.

Too Late

You said you didn't love me
My heart crumbled down
Pieces asked, "how come now?"
All my happiness a swamp
Drowned in aguish

Devil's rope of your words
Cut me so deep I feel numb
Run outside to feel the sadden rain
Just to see my tears disguised
Trying to revive this faded lifeline

Now that you're gone
I try to see the color sky
That's been sprayed with hope
To find I'm in hopelessness
But I can't bring life to what's dead.

Mermaid

I follow your heart like diving into the sea
You're the mermaid of my ocean
Capturing my love with your song
In a whirlpool of your energy
I sink deeper into your magic

Trapped in a bubble you've created
Where my oxygen is romance
Wrap me in all your wonders
In your mythical mysteries
Your kiss becomes my addiction

I would be happy to drown
In the profundity of you
My treasure in uncharted waters
I'm the lost boat searching afar
Until I found you.

Locked

Send me to the unknown curves of your body
Where I can explore happily each work of art
Falling in amazement as I feel heaven in my hands
Your arms cover my back with strength
I start falling into a coma full of ecstasy

My eyes surprised like the first time they had sight
To see so much brilliance created in this world
Each beautiful detail explodes my mind in color
My unworthy fingers blessed to travel around you
Your hot breath tells me silent words of your heart

While your heat melts my thoughts away
I feel my love rising as I hear your heartbeat
Now I know how paradise sounds like
With one gaze, I am forever yours
With one kiss we are locked in this flame.

Composition

You remember the music
Of every dreamt kiss
Every warmed hug
All the melodic looks
How each step forward
The stairs of love
Created an arrangement
That wrote our story
In ink's romance
Impossible to fade
What was made
From passion's
Composition.

No Longer

A promised secret
Waiting to be released
By this longing kiss
The key of one act
To unlock the heart
Of every beginning
Every end of each word
Waking the stars
That rest in your iris
My heart a lighthouse
To your every heartbeat
Once released, no more
Hidden whispers in my lips
My hands no longer tremble
For unspoken written letters
My face no longer looks away
From the star constellation
That lives in my eyes
In the form of you.

Can I Be

Can I be the smile
When you think
Can I be the bridge
Over your waters
Can I be the wings
When you fall
Can I be the patch
To your wounds
Can I be the safe space
When the world falls
Let me be the music
That makes you dance
Let me be the wall
You can lean on
I will be here till the end
I will be your anything
Until your last goodbye.

A Moment

Running to the top of the cliff
To find the edge of the horizon
Where water meets sun
My eyes change view
Through reflecting light scattering
Ocean sounds drag my heart
To cleanse its doubts
Salted air enchants me
Flirting with my face
The sun's temporary goodbye
Brings hope all around me
As my eyes turn back to normal
I hold this moment until my next.

I Will

I will be your guiding light, always
I will hold you even in rain of tears
I will protect you from lurking harm
I will never fall to betrayal's temptations
I will hold your sapphire heart
I will be the fortress of your memory
I will be the sanctuary of your soul
I won't let world's screams bring you down
I will be your sun as you walk the way
I will be your moon if you ever get lost
No matter the running time I will love you
Always.

Discover

Let me soar like an eagle
Free to wander the skies
Discovering every inch
Of this forgotten world
With each find I encounter
My eyes learn new beauty
Eager for the next vision
Trees with stories to tell
As they dance with the wind
I can feel their excitement
Like growing in the ground
Just like them, learning
Absorbing world riches
From the root of life
I'm ready to find
A world that people
Are blind to see.

Melody

The array of light
That pierces me
Reveals the pieces
Needed to complete
The melody of my heart
That wonders sacrifice
For each throb
That it longs for
Creating harmony
That feeds love
To work a piece
So beautiful
It will reach the sky
Where the clouds
Will cry joy
The sun shines
With hopeful warmth
From this musical piece
Composed for you.

Always

Like a mirror reflecting
I don't know if you're real
Maybe an illusion
Swimming in my head
Leaving bubbles of echoes
Pupil full of remembrance
Doubting if anything's real
If I close the doors to my eyes
Will the library in my chest
With all its knowledge of you
Guide me like a blind man
Relying on his senses
The truth I know in me
Is that no matter how
I will always find you.

One Last

Our bodies crumble down
Like wet sand in the face
Of a torn heart falling
Through its final curtains
Severing each life thread
On the path of its torment
Without air in the lungs
To give it a helping hand
All that's left is the sound
Of sorrowful silence
Speaking its last wishes
Before one last beat.

Fox

Like a curious fox
I tinker the world
Loving the forest's
Tranquil sounds
Playing in snow's
Welcoming arms
Making life my den
Gathering skills
From a growing
Footprint left
Behind me
I run forward
synching my breathing
With cutting winds.

Room

I enter the room
To be transported
Into every piece of you
Books of your mind
With every page turned
A new idea full of beauty
The window to light
Reflecting on its glass
A perfect picture of you
At night, the window
Shows me the memories
Of your dreams, staring
At the moonlight
The fragrance left
Comforts me in a wave
That drifts me to you
Closer to your desk
Where adventures fell
From your head
Words traveled
To your hands
To the paper
Where our names
Used to sway
Those days
I used to hold you.

Chapters

In my young age, I would glide the winds
To find you the most beautiful flowers
I would search seas for the purest waters
So I could show you crystal beauties

At middle age, I would build you a castle
To protect you from incoming harm
I would wrap our family in safeties love
In morning, I give you a kiss of honesty

At old age, I appreciate the battles
That made us stronger than tree bark
I love holding your hand as you walk
During disagreements, I wished to be by your side
Because it's clearer than ever that I love you.

Push

When things become hard
The army of perseverance
In you will push through
When anguish falls upon you
The bomb of hope explodes
Propelling you to march forward
Obstacles rise from ground
Unbalancing the odds
Fight with laughter
So the scale is set right
When death comes
Do not quiver
For you have lived
And now, another beginning unfolds.

Left

I will remember the raw love
Spreading out of our hugs
When you said my name
Like soft flowers caressing
How our bodies were like
Fireflies playing, creating light
When you glanced at me
A second passing by
It felt like forever in your eyes
Until the day you spilled me out
With your tears, as the drop fell
Trapped in a watery prison
Until hitting the floor
Where I broke, stretched arm
I saw how you left me.

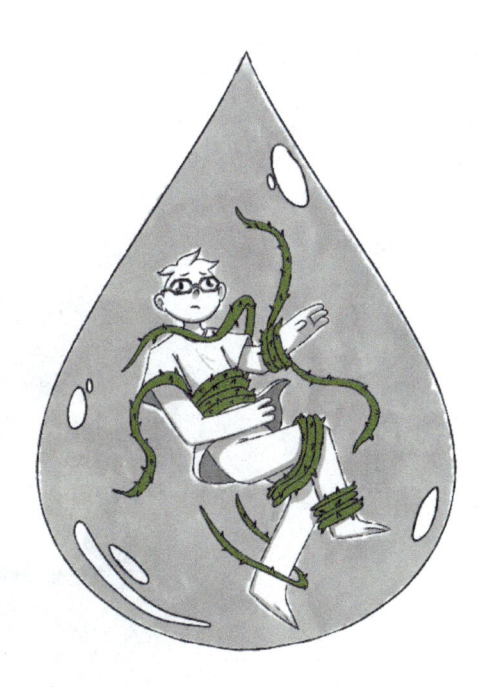

Missing

We search for lifetimes
Feeling like aging faster

Looking for experiences
With gaping holes
Finding their way inside
Just to get lost in a realm
With no explanation

The silence overwhelms
An empty space

Even in the mystery of time
It cannot be filled

Where music is mute

A door impossible to knock
In a place that has no entry

Once closed eyes
I realize
It's forever missing.

Sun

When the fire inside
Is creating its own sun
Flames feel like rising
Through your skin
Fighting forward
Is the only road left
Collapsing down
To unknown ground
Is no option for a sun
Lighting up the path
Of uncertainty
Will be the coal
Giving power
To blazing eyes.

Hands

What marvelous sight
To see growth of hands
Feeling the softness fade
Becoming hardened tools
Carrying life's heavy burden
Lifting up greatest blessings
Withstanding prickly thorns
Of disappointment's grasp
Taking success with delight
Washing new life
Molding routes to walk
How they stretch to give
The way it holds light
When sinking in a wetland
Of second thoughts
How they say goodbye
With a delicate touch.

Moon

My fire is astronomical
Brighter than moonlight
My hope orbits around me
The crazier my ideas are
My desire follows
Like a permanent satellite

Where there's inspiration
I feel my body being pulled
Into a gravitational field
A place of warrior screams
Where giving up is not a word
Dedication the size of a moon

This atmosphere I belong in
Compresses the pressure
Ready to be released
Through sweat and tears
Mind beyond lunar astrology
I know where my fate lies.

At Your Side

At your side paths are pathless
There is only one direction: you
Fragments of your broken heart
Show me the way to your side
Your voice, a siren's call
Irresistible, my heart just flutters

Closer to you I can only feel love
Romance invading my body
Like a virus spreading my cells
This passion is all I breath
Lost shards, I hold at your side
To put together your broken heart.

My Everything

In the cages of my eyes
I find it a blessing
To have you there
Locked in the deepness
Blinded to the world
I can only see you
My everything
The happiness
To my existence

You travel my soul
Use it for warmth
On the coldest parts
Of my heart
Where you have access
To every locked door
My universal key
With just one touch
You are my everything.

My Book

Inspiration on every exhale
I find words for this tale
Nothing would be pale
Our love has no scale
This romance has no fail
Let these letters leave a trail

A dream made in fantasy
Leaving behind any tragedy
These pages have no casualty
Just words of rhapsody
We were perfect alchemy
In this book you are majesty.

No Fear

The lines in my hand a map
That I don't fear to face
It's harder to see as I grow
The roads it shows
Wrinkled and dim
But with fierce will
I get up to follow its trace

Fearless to the storms
That circle my surroundings
Each step made brighter
By the power of my heart
Bringing life to the path
Moving forward from chaos
That fights to bring me down

Like fireflies I'm my own light
Showing the way ahead of me
Bringing peace to the vision
Making my hand firm
To understand the trail
Of this limited adventure
That I will never fear.

Dominating

When I lose control of myself
All my movements are unknown
My senses lost in your breathing
Vision unfocused but focused
That's when I know I'm in love

Your look is penetrating
Finding its way in me
Making me feel illusion
It starts dominating
Every last connection
To this heart you reign.

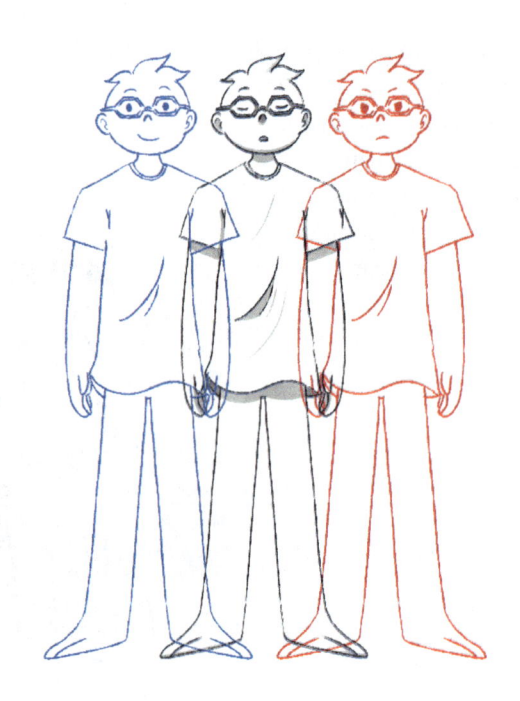

Cost

Seeing you every day had a cost
Me falling in love every moment
Going through the spiral again
Like a never-ending fairytale
Chained to my own heart
A slave to its every command

I was willing to pay the price
No matter what it was
To just be part of your world
Accustomed to this familiar fall
Sometimes afraid that one day
You won't be here in my life

Like passionate lovers
We challenge everything
From fire to lightning
We believe in our love
Like a first spring
Our love seems costless.

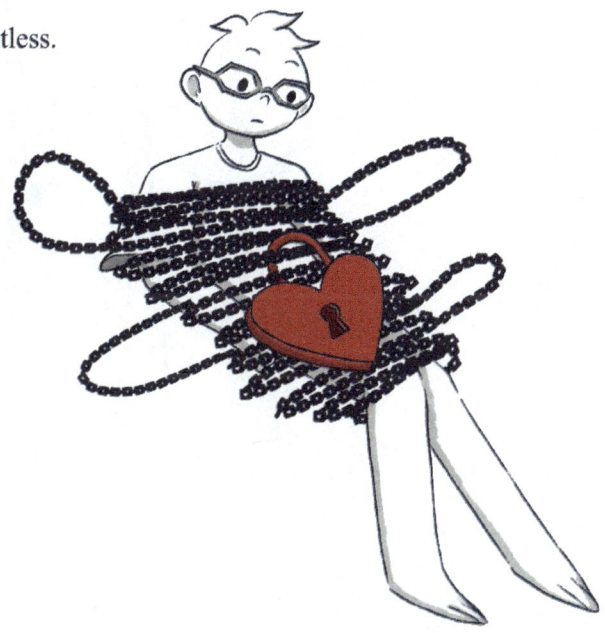

Someday

Every day I wish to be that mirror
Honored to see you until old age
Losing myself in your face is a wish
Hoping you see the reflected love

In the meantime, I wait patiently
A secret kept in the pocket of my heart
Dreaming on a life together
Our souls magnetized when close.

Learning

From the calm movement of earth
My childhood rises like fiery embers
When wind blows, there's tranquility
Adolescence left behind on the shore
In adulthood, tides clash with wisdom

Memories of my eyes projecting
Learning unfolds in this life's movie
With every step, decisions define
Every encounter births experience
I hold the keys to every chapter.

End

What lies await at the end?
A montage of blurred images
Breathing the chill of frozen air

An eternal stroll that stretches on
Towards a shadowed forest's maw
Engulfing us in its enigmatic clutch

An unseen guide leading to a mirage
A distant greeting in the horizon
Only to dissipate like a fleeting dream

The melancholic drop of tears
Holding the weight of all sorrows
A bittersweet testament to our existence

Stitching together shattered hearts
A quilt woven from my own threads
Mending wounds, sharing the pain

Wandering through boundless cosmos
Navigating a labyrinth of memories
Slowly melting away, fading into time

What lies await at the end?
A meadow of dreams fulfilled
Or is it simply the end.

Johnathan Arce Santana

Raised in Puerto Rico, I'm a passionate admirer of the arts, a wanderer captivated by travel's wonders, a dedicated learner, nature's beauty is my sanctuary. A strong believer that words hold the magic to touch hearts and inspire change, making my journey with all the emotions we feel in life become a canvas of creativity and exploration.

Text copyright ©2023 Johnathan Arce Santana.
Illustrations copyright © 2023 Naomi Muñoz Fantauzzi.

All rights reserved. No part of this book may be reproduced or transmitted in any form or by any means, electronic or mechanical, including photocopying, recording, or by any information storage and retrieval system, without written permission from the author.

For information, contact 120DaysofPoetry@gmail.com

ISBN (Paperback): 979-8-8611423-5-9

Made in the USA
Las Vegas, NV
08 October 2023